Exploring Earth's Resources

Using Air

Sharon Katz Cooper

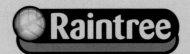

www.raintreepublishers.co.uk

Visit our website to find out more information about **Raintree** books.

To order:

☎ Phone 44 (0) 1865 888112

🖷 Send a fax to 44 (0) 1865 314091

🖳 Visit the Raintree Bookshop at **www.raintreepublishers.co.uk** to browse our catalogue and order online.

First published in Great Britain by Raintree, Halley Court, Jordan Hill, Oxford OX2 8EJ, part of Harcourt Education. Raintree is a registered trademark of Harcourt Education Ltd.

Editorial: Isabel Thomas, Sarah Chappelow and Vicki Yates
Design: Michelle Lisseter
Picture Research: Erica Newbery
Production: Duncan Gilbert

Originated by Modern Age
Printed and bound in China by
  South China Printing Company

10 digit ISBN 1 406 20621 0
13 digit ISBN 978-1-4062-0621-0
11 10 09 08 07
10 9 8 7 6 5 4 3 2 1

British Library Cataloguing in Publication Data
Cooper, Sharon Katz
  Using air. – (Exploring Earth's resources)
  1. Air – Juvenile literature
  I. Title
  333.9'2

ISBN – 13: 9781406206210
ISBN – 10: 1406206210

A full catalogue record for this book is available from the British Library.

Acknowledgements
The publishers would like to thank the following for permission to reproduce photographs: Alamy p. **12** (Travel Ink); Corbis pp. **4** (NASA), **5** (Zefa/ Alexander Benz), **7** (Warren Faidley), **9**, **14** (Walter Geiersperger), **20** (Issei Kato); Getty Images pp. **6** (Iconica), **8** (Photographer's Choice/Brian Stablyk), **10** (Stone), **13** (Photodisc), **15** (Nancy Sefton), **18** (Stone/Jeremy Walker); Harcourt Education Ltd p. **22** (Tudor Photography); Photoedit p. **11** (Tony Freeman); Photolibrary p. **21** (Goodshot); Science Photo Library pp. **16** (British Antarctic Survey), **17** (David Hay Jones); Still Photos p. **19** (Mark Edwards)

Cover photograph reproduced with permission of Getty Images (Stockbyte Silver).

Every effort has been made to contact copyright holders of any material reproduced in this book. Any omissions will be rectified in subsequent printings if notice is given to the publishers.

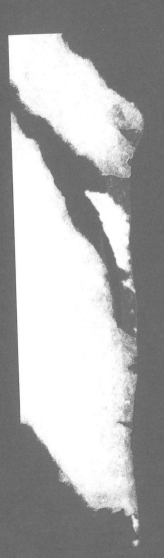

Contents

Some words are shown in bold, **like this**.
You can find them in the glossary on page 23.

What is air?

Air is all around us. Air is a layer
of gases around the Earth.

air bubbles

Air is a **natural resource**.

Natural resources come from
the Earth.

How do we know air is all around us?

We cannot see air, but we can feel it and use it.

We can watch it move a kite.

Wind is air that is moving.

We can see the wind blow trees.

What is air made of?

Air is not nothing. It is a mixture of gases.

Helium is one of the gases in air. We often use it to fill balloons.

Oxygen is an important gas in air. We need it to breathe.

Water **vapour** is another gas in air. Fog is made of water vapour you can see.

How do we use air?

Humans and animals breathe air.

Our bodies need **oxygen** to stay alive.

Air goes into our lungs when we breathe in.

We can blow it out into a balloon.

Plants need air, too.

They use carbon dioxide gas from air to make food.

Plants also put **oxygen** back into air.

Humans and animals need oxygen to breathe.

People use air to make **energy**.
Wind makes windmills turn.

The windmills produce electricity.

We also use air to have fun.

Scuba-divers use tanks of air to dive deep in the ocean.

Who studies air?

Scientists who study air are called meteorologists.

They look at wind and how air moves.

Other scientists study gases and dirt in the air.

They find ways to keep air cleaner.

Can we run out of air?

We cannot run out of air, but air can get dirty.

Using **fossil fuels** causes air **pollution**.

Dirty air can make people ill. It can cause **asthma** and coughing.

How can we keep air clean?

We can help clean our air by burning less **fossil fuel**.

We could drive cleaner cars that use less fuel.

We can sometimes use bikes, buses, and trains instead of cars.

Air experiment

Now you know that we need air to live. Did you know that fire needs air to burn? We use burning for many things, such as cooking and running engines. Try this experiment to see how fire uses up air.

① Light a candle in a holder.

② Place a large glass on top of the candle.

③ Watch to see how long the flame burns.

④ What happened? When the candle has used up the air in the glass, it goes out.

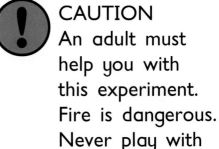

CAUTION
An adult must help you with this experiment. Fire is dangerous. Never play with fire on your own.

Glossary

 **asthma** an illness that makes it hard for a person to breathe

 **energy** something that gives power

 **fossil fuel** gas, oil, or coal. Fossil fuels are made from plants and animals that lived long ago

 **natural resource** a material from the Earth that we can use

 **oxygen** a gas we need to breathe

 **pollution** something that poisons or damages air, water, or land

 **vapour** another word for gas

Index

Titles in the *Exploring Earth's Resources* series include:

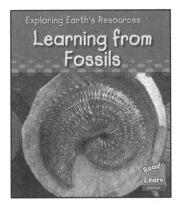

Hardback   1-406-20623-7

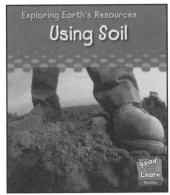

Hardback   1-406-20618-0

Hardback   1-406-20617-2

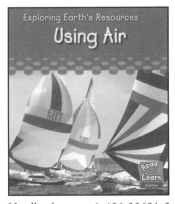

Hardback   1-406-20621-0

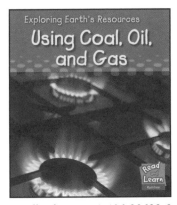

Hardback   1-406-20622-9

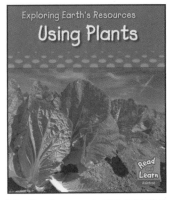

Hardback   1-406-20619-9

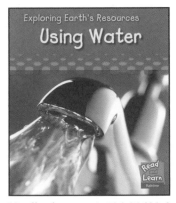

Hardback   1-406-20620-2

Find out about the other titles in this series on our website www.raintreepublishers.co.uk